ANIMAL WORLD

THE FASTEST ANIMALS IN THE WORLD

by Samantha S. Bell

BrightPoint Press

San Diego, CA

LIBRARY OF CONGRESS CATALOGING-IN-PUBLICATION DATA

Names: Bell, Samantha S., author.
Title: The fastest animals in the world / by Samantha S. Bell.
Description: San Diego, CA: BrightPoint Press, [2024] | Series: Animal world | Includes
   bibliographical references and index. | Audience: Ages 13 | Audience: Grades 7-9
Identifiers: LCCN 2023004141 (print) | LCCN 2023004142 (eBook) | ISBN 9781678206161
   (hardcover) | ISBN 9781678206178 (eBook)
Subjects: LCSH: Animals--Speed--Juvenile literature. | Animal locomotion--Juvenile
   literature.
Classification: LCC QL49 .B377 2024 (print) | LCC QL49 (eBook) | DDC 591.47/9--dc23/
   eng/20230324
LC record available at https://lccn.loc.gov/2023004141
LC eBook record available at https://lccn.loc.gov/2023004142

CONTENTS

AT A GLANCE

- The fastest animals in the world often use their speed to hunt prey.

- The cheetah is the fastest land animal on Earth. It can run at almost 70 miles per hour (113 kmh).

- The cheetah is perfectly built for running. Its skeleton, muscles, and senses make it a swift hunter.

- The peregrine falcon is the fastest animal on Earth. It dives at speeds of 200 miles per hour (322 kmh) or more.

- The peregrine falcon uses its strong eyesight, streamlined body, and precise navigational senses to snatch its prey out of the air.

- One of the fastest swimmers on Earth is the sailfish. It can lower its huge fin to make itself more streamlined. It uses its speed to hunt fish.

- Overfishing and pollution threaten the future of sailfish. Even when the fish are returned to the water after being caught, they're affected by the ordeal for hours.

- The American badger is one of the fastest diggers on Earth. It can dig itself out of sight in just three minutes.

- Badgers have long, curved claws that they use to loosen soil. They throw the excess dirt behind them and continue digging.

INTRODUCTION

FANTASTIC FLYER

High above the streets of New York City, a peregrine falcon looks for its next meal. It perches near its nesting box at the top of a tall bridge. A pigeon flies toward a statue near the waterfront. The falcon's keen eyes spot the pigeon about 1 mile (1.6 km) away. The falcon takes to the air.

Suddenly, it pulls in its wings and hurls itself toward the pigeon. The falcon reaches a speed of 200 miles per hour (322 kmh). This nosedive, called a stoop, surprises the pigeon. The falcon snatches the pigeon

Peregrine falcons have see-through eyelids that they close when they're flying at high speeds. This protects their eyes from dust and wind.

Peregrine falcons mate for life. They tend to nest together in the same place every year.

out of the air. Within moments, the falcon is

heading back to its nest.

The pigeon will provide a good meal for

the falcon. But the city is not the falcon's

usual habitat. In nature, falcons will nest and perch on high cliffs. The cliffs give them a good view for spotting prey. But falcons can adapt to many different environments. Skyscrapers and bridges in cities provide the same high views as cliffs.

AMAZING ANIMALS

Peregrine falcons are the fastest animals in the world. But many other amazing animals also use their speed every day. Some soar above buildings. Others swim in the ocean. Some run over land. Still others live underground.

Speed is used for different purposes. Some animals use their speed to catch prey. Others use it to escape predators. A few use it to build shelters.

Every animal uses its talents a little differently. But for many of them, speed is an important part of their survival. But survival can be tricky. Animals all over the world are being faced with new threats. Humans are causing many of these threats. Pollution and habitat loss are harming many species. Conservation work is needed to keep these speedy animals safe.

Rehabilitation, conservation, and education are all important parts of protecting the world's fastest species.

1

CHEETAHS

Cheetahs live in the grasslands of Africa and Asia. They are the world's fastest land animals. These wild cats are different from other big cats. They cannot roar like lions, tigers, and leopards. Instead, they make a chirping sound.

Cheetahs have rough fur. Their **tawny** coats are speckled with solid black blotches. This helps them blend in with tall grasses. They use this camouflage to sneak up on their prey. Cheetahs also have black

Cheetahs are fantastic at catching prey but not as good at keeping it. About 10 percent of the prey they kill is stolen by other predators.

lines on their faces. The lines run from their eyes down to their chins. Scientists believe these dark marks may help reduce the glare of the sun.

Cheetahs hunt alone. This means they must choose prey they can catch by themselves. Cheetahs eat birds, rabbits, and antelope. They also eat the young of larger animals, such as warthogs and

STILL HOLDING THE RECORD

The top cheetah speed was recorded in 1965. Trainers taught a tame female cheetah in Kenya to run behind a car. The cheetah ran a 656-foot (200-m) straight course three times. The average of her three runs was 63.7 miles per hour (102.5 kmh).

wildebeests. Cheetahs can **accelerate** to 45 miles per hour (72 kmh) in just 2.5 seconds. Their top speeds average between 60 and 70 miles per hour (97–113 kmh).

BUILT FOR SPEED

From head to tail, a cheetah's body is designed for speed. Its bones are lightweight. It does not have as much weight to carry as other big cats. Its collarbone is smaller than those of other cats. Its shoulder blades are vertical and not attached to the collarbone. This allows the cheetah to lengthen its stride and accelerate quickly.

The cheetah's spine, or backbone, is the longest and most flexible of the big cats. As the cheetah runs, its spine acts as a coiled spring. Luke Hunter is the president of Panthera, an organization that helps wild cats. He describes how the cheetah's spine affects its speed. He says, "It enables the cheetah to maximize the stride length. By bunching and coiling the spine alone, it's able to expand this incredible stride rate."[1] At top speed, a cheetah can advance 23 feet (7 m) in a single stride.

A cheetah's muscles contain many fast-twitch fibers. These muscle fibers are built for short bursts of energy. They give the cheetah the explosive power for its fast start.

A cheetah's feet and tail also help it in the chase. A cheetah has tough pads on the bottom of its feet. These pads give it maximum traction. Unlike other big cats, it has blunt claws. A cheetah's claws do

BURST OF SPEED

Cheetahs can run really fast, but they can't keep those speeds up for very long. Cheetahs usually sprint for less than a minute at a time.

Baby cheetahs are called cubs. Mother cheetahs teach their cubs how to hunt.

not **retract** all the way. They work like an

athlete's cleats, giving the cheetah extra

traction, or grip. A cheetah's tail acts as

a rudder. It helps the cheetah make fast

turns. Cathryn Hilker founded the Cat

Ambassador Program at the Cincinnati Zoo. She says, "This is the cat that is utter perfection for what he does. He does nothing but run."[2]

EYES ON THE PRIZE

As a cheetah runs, its legs, back, and muscles make powerful movements. But its head hardly moves at all. It locks its eyes on its prey. Its eyes stay fixed on its target even at high speeds. This is because of the cheetah's unique hunting adaptations.

The cheetah's skull is smaller and lighter than those of other big cats. This makes it more **streamlined**. The cheetah's eyes are higher on its head than those of other cats. This lets the cheetah see a wider area. The **retinas** in its eyes have an elongated shape. This gives the cheetah a sharp, wide-angled view of its surroundings. It can spot its prey up to 3 miles (5 km) away.

The shape of a cheetah's head helps in another way. Its skull is shorter than those of other big cats. This allows it to have a bigger **nasal cavity**. This lets cheetahs take more air into their large lungs. Having extra air helps them breathe more easily while running. A cheetah takes about sixty

Cheetahs are crepuscular. This means that they mainly hunt at dawn and dusk.

breaths per minute when resting. It takes about 150 breaths per minute when running at full speed.

Cheetahs also have specially adapted structures in their inner ears. The inner ears of mammals help them keep their balance. It also helps them keep their head steady as they move. A cheetah's inner ears give it greater sensitivity and faster responses to head movements. This helps it keep its vision stable and fixed on its prey.

RUNNING INTO PROBLEMS

Cheetahs are natural predators. But cheetahs are also the ones in danger. In 2022, only about 6,500 cheetahs lived in the wild. Humans are their biggest threat. Sometimes cheetahs are hunted for sport. Cubs are captured as pets. Other cheetahs suffer habitat loss as people use their land for farming. People will sometimes

Cheetahs have disappeared from most of their land. Today, they occupy only 9 percent of their former territory.

kill cheetahs if they believe their own animals are threatened. Conservationists are working hard to find new ways to keep these amazing cats running free.

2

PEREGRINE FALCONS

The peregrine falcon is the fastest animal on Earth. This bird can reach speeds of more than 200 miles per hour (322 kmh). That's as fast as a race car.

Peregrine falcons live on every continent except Antarctica. They feed on a wide variety of birds depending on where they live. In cities, peregrine falcons eat

pigeons and songbirds. Along the coasts

and waterways, they eat ducks, gulls,

geese, and shorebirds. Sometimes the

Peregrine falcons may eat as many as 2,000 different species of birds.

falcons will also eat small mammals, reptiles, and insects.

Because peregrine falcons eat so many different types of birds, they can live in almost any type of climate and habitat. They can be found in deserts, wetlands, and grasslands. They make homes in forests, mountains, and cities. Although these habitats are very different, they all have good nesting locations.

Peregrine falcons hunt in several different ways. Sometimes they chase their prey through the air. Flapping their wings, they reach speeds of up to 65 miles per hour (105 kmh). Other times, they dive from high above. First they use their strong eyesight to locate birds flying below. When the falcon finds its target, it folds its wings close to its body and falls into a nosedive toward the prey. Sometimes the falcon grabs its prey. Other times, it knocks the prey out of the sky.

WHAT'S IN A NAME?

The word *peregrine* comes from a Latin word that means traveler. Peregrine falcons were given this name because of the long migrations they make.

MADE FOR SPEED

Some birds have a breastbone specialized for flight. This bone is called a keel. The muscles birds use for flapping their wings are attached to the keel. The size of the keel determines a bird's flying ability. The peregrine falcon has a very large keel. This allows more muscles to be attached to it.

DIVING TOGETHER

Ken Franklin works with a peregrine falcon named Frightful. Franklin wanted to measure the bird's speed in mid-dive. To do this, he had to dive with her. Franklin has done more than 200 skydives with Frightful. She has been clocked at 242 miles per hour (389 kmh).

These extra muscles let the falcon produce more flapping power.

The peregrine falcon's wings are designed for speed too. They have slim, stiff feathers that are unslotted. This means they do not spread out at the end of the wing. Hawks and eagles have slotted feathers. Slotted feathers help increase gliding ability. But they cause birds to experience **drag** as the wind pulls on their feathers. The peregrine falcon does not have this problem. Its wings come to sharp tips at the ends. It folds them in close to its body as it dives. This lets it cut through the air easily.

Peregrine falcons also have plenty of red muscle fibers. Red muscle fibers increase oxygen. The falcons' red muscle fibers help the birds fly longer. Peregrine falcons also have large, strong hearts that beat up to 900 times per minute. This pumps oxygen through their blood even while flying at high speeds. If other birds flew this fast, they would not be able to breathe.

STAYING ON TARGET

Scientists have spent years trying to understand how the peregrine falcon hunts. It dives at extreme speeds. Yet it does not

Peregrine falcons aren't just fast; they also have great endurance. Some migrate 15,500 miles (25,000 km) every year.

hurt itself. And it rarely misses its target.

Recent studies show that the falcon has its

own navigational system. This system is a

lot like that of a missile.

Peregrine falcon nests aren't fancy. Their nests are simple scratches in the dirt on a roof or cliff edge.

Missiles are guided with proportional navigation. Instead of staying on a straight course, missiles make adjustments as they go. Peregrine falcons do the same thing. As they dive toward their prey, they make slight changes in wing position and speed. Graham Taylor is a professor of Mathematical Biology at Oxford University in England. He says, "Falcons aren't doing complicated **computations** to figure out where the target is going to be, but the behavior that you see almost looks as if they do."[3]

EMPTY SKIES

It is difficult to imagine a world without these amazing fliers. But peregrine falcons were once on the brink of extinction. After World War II (1939–1945), farmers began using a dangerous chemical called DDT. They used DDT to kill insects. This chemical poisoned a lot of natural resources. Smaller birds were eating seeds and insects tainted with DDT. Falcons ate the birds and were exposed to DDT too. Although DDT did not kill the falcons, it made their eggshells too thin. The eggs broke when the parents sat on them. New chicks weren't able to hatch. By 1970, peregrine falcons were listed as endangered in the United States.

In 1972, DDT was banned in the United States. Conservationists and concerned citizens began helping the falcons. They bred falcons in captivity and helped raise the young. Then they created nesting sites on top of power plants, office buildings,

Peregrine falcon mates take care of their chicks together. They bring the chicks food, keep them warm, and protect them from predators.

and factories. They watched over the nests

to make sure the chicks were doing well.

Because of this help, peregrine falcons have

made a comeback.

3

SAILFISH

The sailfish is one of the fastest swimmers in the world. It can be found in tropical ocean waters. The sailfish is part of a group of species known as billfish. Billfish have long, spear-like upper jaws, or bills. These bills have small, toothlike projections on the sides.

It's easy to tell the sailfish apart from other billfish. The sailfish gets its name from the huge dorsal fin on its back. The fin is almost as long as the sailfish's body. This fin is kept folded down and to one side.

Though sailfish normally stay near the surface, they can dive up to 1,150 feet (350 m) to find prey.

The fish will raise it if it feels threatened or excited. This makes the fish appear bigger.

Sailfish can grow up to 10 feet (3 m) long. They can weigh up to 220 pounds (100 kg). The top of the fish is blue. The lower part is white with rows of light blue dots. However, its color may change depending on how excited it is.

The sailfish can swim at speeds of up to 70 miles per hour (113 kmh). Its streamlined body helps it reach these speeds. When it folds its large fin back, it's shaped like a torpedo. This shape helps reduce drag as the fish cuts through the water. The scales on its skin help too. Their unusual shape causes the fish to be wrapped in a bubble of air. The air is lighter than the dense water. This helps the fish move even faster.

WORKING TOGETHER

Sailfish are among the top predators of the open ocean. They mostly feed during

AS SLEEK AS A SAILFISH

Frank Stephenson is the design director of McLaren Automotive. The company designs expensive sports cars. He was inspired by how fast sailfish swim. He saw that the texture of their scales made them move more swiftly through the water. He lined the inside of air ducts with this texture, allowing them to quickly pump air to cool engines. The result was the McLaren P1 hybrid supercar.

the day. Smaller fish such as anchovies and sardines make up most of their diet. They also eat larger fish that swim near the surface. This includes tuna, mackerel, and herring. Sometimes sailfish eat other ocean creatures, such as squids and octopuses.

Sailfish use group hunting strategies when they hunt schools of fish. First they surround a school of smaller fish. Then they raise their tall fins to herd the fish into a tight ball. They will often move the school toward the surface of the water.

Once the school is gathered, the sailfish burst through it. They move their long bills

Up to forty sailfish can hunt together at a time.

from side to side. The bills slash through

the group of small fish. This cuts and

stuns them. The sailfish can then leisurely

eat their meal.

Sailfish do not rely solely on their speed

to hunt. They also rely on their bills and the

accuracy of their movements. A sailfish

may gently ease its bill into the school of fish. The large sail helps the sailfish limit the movement of the water. The small fish don't even notice. The sailfish then moves its bill back and forth and grabs its prey.

HIDDEN DANGERS

Sailfish are high on the food chain. They have few predators. But that does not

RACE FOR ROMANCE

Male sailfish use their speed to get mates. During mating season, male sailfish often compete for the same partner. They will race each other to see who gets the female. Whoever reaches the female first wins.

mean they're safe. Sailfish are among the most popular sport fish. Fishers enjoy the high-energy challenge of catching them. Most of the time, fishers will catch the fish and then release them. But the fish are still affected by the battle.

Ryan Logan is a research associate at Nova Southeastern University. He studied how long it takes the sailfish to recover after being caught. He explains that for the fish, "this is a fight for its life using a tremendous amount of energy."[4] Logan found that it takes the fish about five hours to recover from the stress.

Like many marine animals, sailfish must deal with pollution. When people are fishing, they will sometimes leave their equipment behind in the water. This abandoned equipment is known as ghost gear. It continues to catch fish even after being discarded. Sailfish are often trapped and killed by this gear. But they aren't the only animals impacted by this pollution. More than 650,000 animals are killed by ghost gear every year. Fishers, companies, and concerned citizens can all help reduce this trash in the oceans by cleaning up their gear.

TOP SPEEDS

Peregrine falcon: 240 miles per hour (386 kmh)[1]

Cheetah: 70 miles per hour (113 kmh)[2]

Sailfish: 70 miles per hour (113 kmh)[1]

Average highway speed in the United States: 69.8 miles per hour (112 kmh)[3]

1. Regina Bailey, "The Fastest Animals on the Planet," ThoughtCo, January 28, 2019. www.thoughtco.com.

2. Hannah Lang, "Now Scientists Can Accurately Guess the Speed of Any Animal," National Geographic, July 17, 2017. www.nationalgeographic.com.

3. "USA Speed Limits by State," Rhino Car Hire, n.d. www.rhinocarhire.com.

Some animals are built for speed. They can move faster than cars on a highway.

4

AMERICAN BADGERS

Some animals make their homes underground. Among them is the American badger. The badger digs dens and tunnels. It is one of the fastest digging animals. A badger can dig itself out of sight in three minutes or less. It can dig faster than two people using shovels. It is such a strong digger that it can even dig through concrete and pavement.

The American badger is the only species of badger that lives in North America. These badgers make their homes from northern

North American badgers are nocturnal. This means they sleep during the day and are active at night.

Mexico to southern Canada. In the United States, they can be found in central and western states.

The badger has a broad body with a muscular neck and short, powerful legs. Its fur is silver-gray or tan. It has a white stripe that runs from its nose over the top of its head. Adult badgers grow to be about 22 to 28 inches (56–71 cm) long.

The badger's favorite habitats include treeless areas such as prairies, meadows, and grasslands. They can be found along the edges of forests too. These habitats provide them with sandy soils that are good for digging. Areas with a lot of trees have roots that are harder to dig through.

NECESSARY SKILLS

Badgers usually live alone. Mother badgers are the exception to this. Females will live with their babies for about five to six months until the young can take care of themselves.

Badgers live in dens. They dig their dens for protection. The den provides a safe

BABY BADGERS

Baby badgers are normally born in March. They're born blind. After six weeks, they open their eyes and can explore outside their dens. They stay with their mothers for about six months.

Before a female badger gives birth, she will dig out a den and line it with grass. Her babies are called cubs.

place for the badger to sleep. A badger may dig a new den every couple of days. In the summertime, male badgers and females without young change dens often. During the winter, badgers settle into a single den to shelter from the cold.

The opening of a badger's den is about 10 to 12 inches (25–30 cm) wide. Some dens go as far as 10 feet (3 m) underground. The den includes a sleeping chamber and tunnels that can be 20 to 30 feet (6–9 m) long.

Badgers also dig to find food. Badgers are carnivores, or meat eaters. But they eat whatever they find. Sometimes they eat plants such as corn or berries. They will also eat bird eggs, frogs, snakes, and insects. They will even eat **carrion**. But much of their diet is made up of other burrowing mammals. These include woodchucks, ground squirrels, voles, and gophers.

Most of the time, burrows are places of safety for animals. But this changes if a badger is on the hunt. To capture their prey, badgers will chase a prey animal into its burrow. The badger then digs down

BURIED BY A BADGER

Biologist Evan Buechley left the carcass of a cow in the desert. He wanted to film the animals that ate it. A badger dug around the cow until it fell into a pit. Then it covered it up. Beuchley says, "So it worked overtime for five days, like really, really intensely, and then it just had a two-week feeding fest."

Merrit Kennedy, "VIDEO: Badger Burying A Cow Surprises Scientists," NPR, April 4, 2017. www.npr.org.

after it and traps the animal underground. Some burrows have more than one entrance, giving the animal an escape route. But badgers sometimes block these entrances before going after their prey.

A DIGGING MACHINE

Badgers are built for digging quickly. The curved claws on their front feet are 2 inches (5 cm) long. The claws loosen the soil and pass it backward. Their back paws have short, shovellike claws. The claws fling the dirt behind the badger as it digs. Biologist Barbara Ver Steeg studied American badgers for many years. She says, "At high speeds, a tunneling badger throws a plume of dirt into the air behind it."[5]

Badgers are suited for digging in another way. They have see-through inner eyelids. These eyelids are called nictitating membranes. As they dig, the badgers cover their eyes with the membranes. The membranes protect the badgers' eyes from dust and dirt.

Badgers are an important part of the ecosystem. They help keep down the rodent population. Their digging activities help improve the soil by bringing air into it.

A badger will have a pile of dirt next to its den entrance. When it's threatened by a predator, it can quickly use the dirt to plug up the hole to its den. This lets the badger escape danger.

Their empty burrows are used by many other animals, including burrowing owls and rattlesnakes.

BYE BYE BADGERS?

Even though badgers do not have many natural predators, their numbers are

One way people can help protect badgers is by growing native plants, like tall grasses. These plants provide good habitats for badgers and their prey.

decreasing. One of the biggest threats

to their survival is loss of habitat. Homes,

cities, and farms have taken over land

where badgers live. Roads cut through the badgers' habitats. This causes many badgers to be hit by cars. In Canada, the American badger is an endangered species. People can protect badgers by protecting their habitats.

Cheetahs, peregrine falcons, sailfish, and American badgers are some of the fastest animals in the world. Their bodies are built for speed. They are top predators. But they still face threats from humans. Their habitats are being destroyed. By understanding these animals and what they can do, people will be able to better help them.

GLOSSARY

accelerate
to increase in speed

carrion
a dead or rotting animal

computations
mathematical calculations

drag
a force that opposes the motion of an object through the air

nasal cavity
the inside of the nose

retinas
the parts of eyes that sense light and color

retract
to pull back in

streamlined
offering minimum resistance when moving through air or water

tawny
an orange-brown or yellow-brown color

SOURCE NOTES

CHAPTER ONE: CHEETAHS

1. Quoted in "The Science of a Cheetah's Speed," *YouTube*, uploaded by National Geographic, May 8, 2013. www.youtube.com.

2. Quoted in "The Science of a Cheetah's Speed."

CHAPTER TWO: PEREGRINE FALCONS

3. Quoted in Rebecca Hersher, "Peregrine Falcons Attack Like Missiles to Grab Prey Midair, Scientists Find," *NPR*, December 4, 2017. www.npr.org.

CHAPTER THREE: SAILFISH

4. Quoted in Keegan Sentner, "How Long Does It Take a Billfish to Recover After It's Caught and Released?" *Outdoor Life*, August 24, 2022. www.outdoorlife.com.

CHAPTER FOUR: AMERICAN BADGERS

5. Quoted in Les Line, "The Benefit of Badgers," *National Wildlife Federation*, December 1, 1995. www.nwf.org.

FOR FURTHER RESEARCH

BOOKS

Dereck and Beverly Joubert and Suzanne Zimbler, *The Ultimate Book of African Animals*. Washington, DC: National Geographic Kids, 2021.

Karen McGhee, *World's Most Extreme Animals*. New York: Gareth Stevens Publishing, 2022.

Philip Wolny, *The Deadliest Animals in the World*. San Diego, CA: BrightPoint Press, 2023.

INTERNET SOURCES

"Cheetah," *National Geographic,* n.d. www.nationalgeographic.com.

Monica Cull, "What You Need to Know About Sailfish," *Discover Magazine,* August 1, 2022. www.discovermagazine.com.

Michelle Durant and Katherine Young, "Nature Detectives: Dig Badger Dig," *Boulder County, CO*, February 28, 2014. https://bouldercounty.gov.

WEBSITES

All About Birds - The Cornell Lab
www.allaboutbirds.org

All About Birds, a website run by Cornell University, has information and photos about hundreds of bird species.

Memphis Zoo
www.memphiszoo.org

The Memphis Zoo is located in Memphis, Tennessee. Its website includes live videos of its animals and information about a wide range of species.

Panthera
https://panthera.org

Founded in 2006, Panthera was created to protect the world's wild cats and their habitats. The organization's website has information about all forty species of wild cats.

INDEX

IMAGE CREDITS

ABOUT THE AUTHOR

Samantha S. Bell has written more than 130 nonfiction books for kids. She lives with her family in the foothills of the Blue Ridge Mountains, where she enjoys learning about the animals that live in the woods around them. She's seen chipmunks, squirrels, rabbits, deer, foxes, skunks, opossums, groundhogs, coyotes, bobcats, and black bears.